# MAKE IT
## WITH
# HART

Piccolo Books

# Making It With Hart

This is a book about making things. Some sensible, some quite silly, but all of them designed for you to make at home or at school with enthusiasm and the minimum of expense. Most of the materials you can pick up at home – things that are going to be thrown away, like plastic cups, boxes, cardboard tubes, wrapping material, and so on. Sometimes you'll want to work on your own. You'll find plenty of projects for that. At other times you can get the gang working together. Then again, some bigger jobs can be undertaken by a class, of any age, at school. In the book you can see just what happens then!

You'll find that most of these ideas can be taken further. If you are creative, mechanical, artistic, or just plain interested, you will want to add your own imaginative ideas. I hope you will. So get together all the interesting odds and ends that you think might be useful – and start making it with Hart.

# Contents

Landscaping **6**
Flower Pots **8**
Bird Table **9**
Tie Dyeing **10**
Mobile Art **12**
Windmill **14**
Sponge Painting **15**
Mad Masks **16**
Fun at the Fair **17**
Doll's House Furniture **20**
Egging You On **22**
Scrap Art **24**
Tree House **26**
Action Painting **28**
Chess Men **31**
Puppet Shows **32**
Tee! Hee! Shirts **34**
Wire Sculptures **36**
Beach Art **38**
Polystyrenia **40**
Treasure Chests **41**
Ring Pull Curtains **42**
Thong Things **43**
Coalminer Doll **44**
Pulp Art **46**
Merry Christmas Decorations **48**

Front Cover Photograph by Tony Evans.
Inside Photography by Tony Hart and Phil Sayer.

The publishers would like to thank the Headmistresses and the Children of Highgate Primary School (Infants) and Shamley Green Primary School for their help on the Action Painting and Sponge Art sections of this book. Thanks also to Gary, Adam, Rebecca, Emily-Alice, Edmond, Zoë, Caitlin, Ian, Edward, Joanna and Rebecca for their help on the Beach Art.

# Making the Rules

**1.** Read the instructions carefully before you start to make anything and get all the materials together first. These signs tell you which basic tools you need:

**2.** Make sure your scissors and craft knife are sharp. Sharp means **safe** – as long as you keep your fingers well behind the blade, and concentrate on what you're doing. Look out for this danger sign:

**3.** When painting or plastering, make certain you are wearing your oldest clothes, and that the floor, table or whatever is well covered with newspaper etc.

**4.** Clear up any mess after you've finished.

**5.** Some things are harder to make than others. If you don't get it right first time – try again. If you're really stuck, get someone to help you.

# Landscaping

Build your own countryside

You need: a board for the base (hardboard is fine), as big as you like; sand; cardboard; lots of newspaper; wallpaper paste; plaster of paris.

**1.** Cut out 3 card walls and stick around edge of board. Then pour in damp sand. Shape into hills, valleys, river etc.

**2.** Tear newspaper into smallish pieces, brush with paste, and lay carefully all over sand. Keep adding newspaper until papier mâché is as thick as cardboard. Leave to dry for about 2 days.

**3.** Mix plaster, brush over papier mâché – but not on rivers or sea. Before it sets, comb in ploughed fields etc. Scrape out roads with flat card.

When dry, paint with poster paints – use gloss for water.

**4.** Remove one wall to empty out sand.

**5.** Make trees with foam rubber or use real twigs.

**6.** Build bridges and houses with cardboard (cut out doors and windows) – then paint.

# Flower Pots

Any plastic pot makes a suitable base for decoration. You can grow things in them outside or indoors.

1. Cut slits, same distance apart, down length of pot. Paint with modelling or emulsion paint.

2. From thin plastic or other plastic cups, cut ribbons same width as pot slits – and long enough to go right round. Paint a different colour.

3. Thread plastic ribbons through slits as shown.

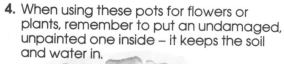

4. When using these pots for flowers or plants, remember to put an undamaged, unpainted one inside – it keeps the soil and water in.

# Bird Table

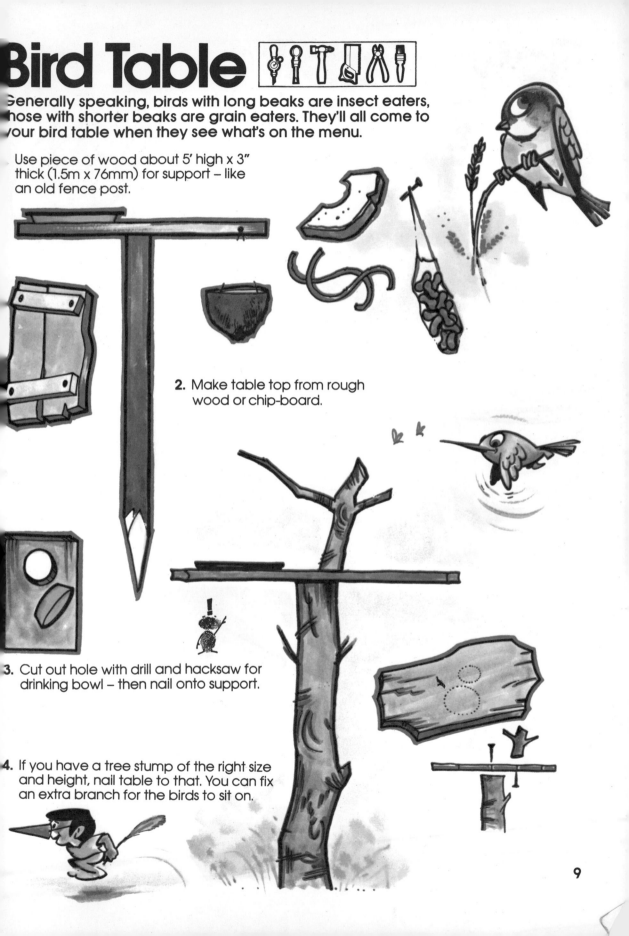

Generally speaking, birds with long beaks are insect eaters, those with shorter beaks are grain eaters. They'll all come to your bird table when they see what's on the menu.

1. Use piece of wood about 5' high x 3" thick (1.5m x 76mm) for support – like an old fence post.

2. Make table top from rough wood or chip-board.

3. Cut out hole with drill and hacksaw for drinking bowl – then nail onto support.

4. If you have a tree stump of the right size and height, nail table to that. You can fix an extra branch for the birds to sit on.

9

# Tie Dyeing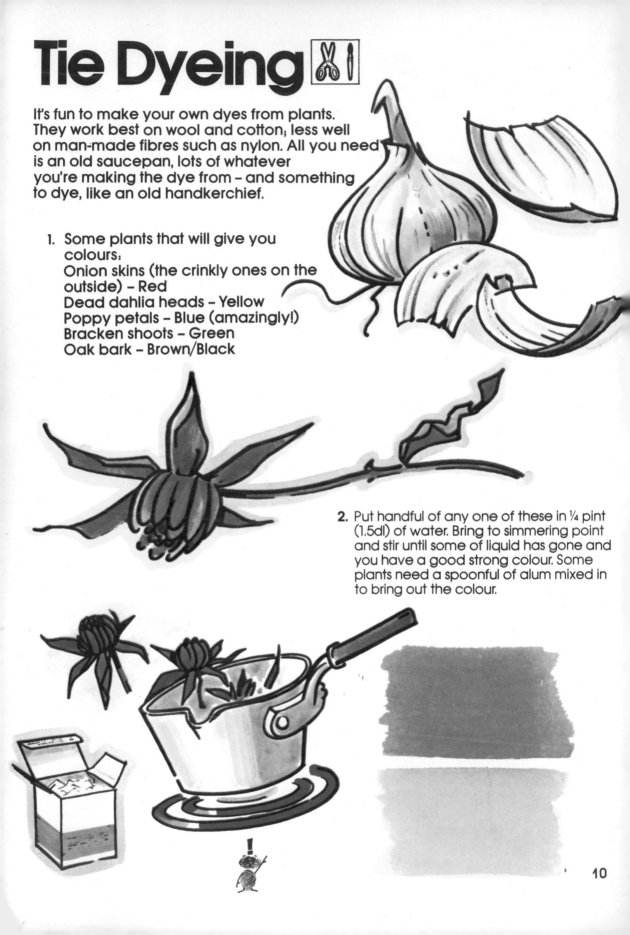

It's fun to make your own dyes from plants. They work best on wool and cotton, less well on man-made fibres such as nylon. All you need is an old saucepan, lots of whatever you're making the dye from – and something to dye, like an old handkerchief.

1. Some plants that will give you colours:
   Onion skins (the crinkly ones on the outside) – Red
   Dead dahlia heads – Yellow
   Poppy petals – Blue (amazingly!)
   Bracken shoots – Green
   Oak bark – Brown/Black

2. Put handful of any one of these in ¼ pint (1.5dl) of water. Bring to simmering point and stir until some of liquid has gone and you have a good strong colour. Some plants need a spoonful of alum mixed in to bring out the colour.

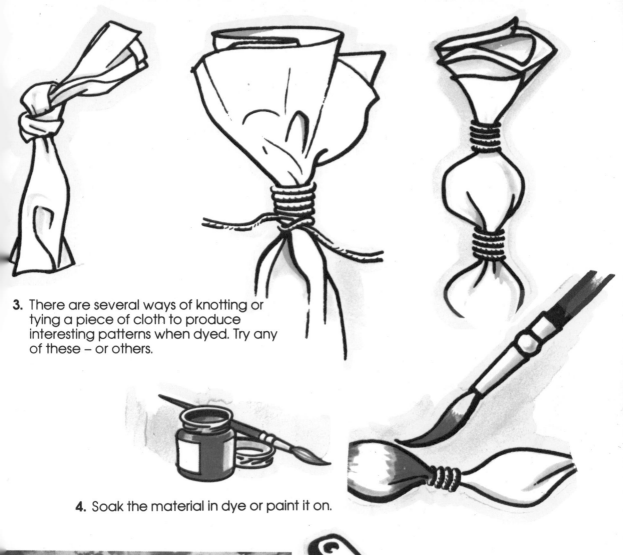

3. There are several ways of knotting or tying a piece of cloth to produce interesting patterns when dyed. Try any of these – or others.

4. Soak the material in dye or paint it on.

5. If you don't want to make your own dye, you can buy one of the vegetable or chemical varieties. And carry on from there.

**11**

# Mobile Art

A mobile is a sculpture that moves. Most mobiles hang from the ceiling, but you can also make them for standing up.

Mobiles must balance. You do this by adding a bit to one of the forms, or taking a bit away. Moving wires or threads can also help. Steel wire is the best.

**1.** Paint cardboard shapes.

Use cardboard, wood, or modelling clay to make the forms.

**2.** Fasten wire with sticky tape.

**3.** Ping-pong balls on wire.

**4.** Modelling clay.

**5.** Stick pencil into wooden base (drill holes) – and fix cardboard shapes on top.

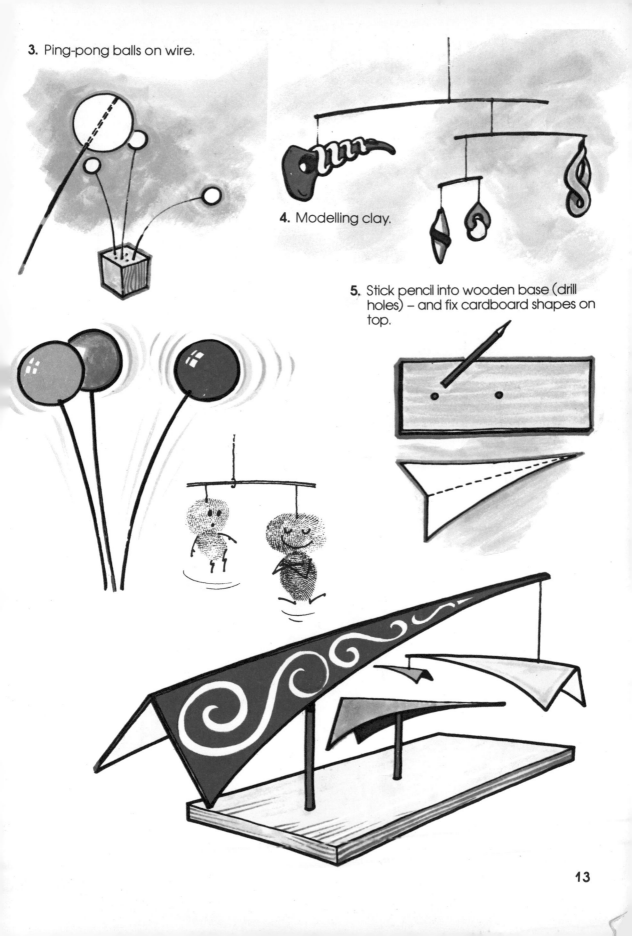

# Windmill

When you've made a windmill put it into your model landscape – it will look terrific.

1. Use empty detergent bottle **or** 3″ (76mm) cardboard tube **or** plastic cups for the mill tower.

2. Make 4 sails with strips of cardboard. Cut 4 slits in cotton reel with hacksaw. (Get someone to do this for you if you are not used to carpentry.)

3. If using plastic cups, put roll of card inside each one for extra height.

4. Make a small hole at top of tower, back and front. Slot pencil or dowling rod through to hold sails. Put a second cotton reel at the back for balance. Attach weight (a piece of modelling clay or another reel) as shown.

5. To make really firm, stick base or square of cardboard.

# Sponge Painting

Giant pictures for the wall or floor. Always use emulsion paint.
Mix in trays or on large sheets of polythene.

The idea is to paint pictures without brushes. Any sort of
sponge will do – just dab or roll the paint on.

**1.** If you want something to grip, stick the
sponge onto a fairly thick piece of board
with latex adhesive.

**2.** Cardboard holder
for thin sponge.

**3.** Cut out any shape, any size.

# Mad Masks

Ideal for parties or hiding from your friends. Remember to take it off before you go to sleep – you don't want to scare your mother when she comes to say goodnight!

**1.** Start with roll of thin card, big enough to cover your head. Don't make it so tight it hurts your ears!

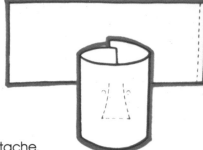

**2.** Cut out holes for eyes and flap for nose.

**3.** Eyebrows, beard, moustache.

**4.** Horns and teeth.

**5.** Hair and hat.

**6.** Frankenstein's monster.

**7.** Paint with bright poster colours.

# Fun at the Fair

Make your own fairground – then treat your friends to a visit.
Cut and stick everything together very carefully with an
all-purpose adhesive. Paint in very bright colours.

## Slide

Make it big enough to race your cars down.

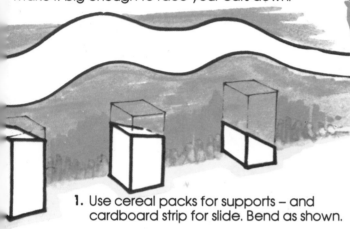

**1.** Use cereal packs for supports – and
cardboard strip for slide. Bend as shown.

**2.** Stick on narrow strips either side for walls.

## Helter-Skelter

1. Cut spiral shape from card –
   so it springs up.
2. Cut and slot together 2 triangles
   for top piece.

**3.** Make cone from cartridge paper or thin
card – and wrap spiral around.

17

# Carousel

**1.** Cut cardboard to shape – slot one on top of the other.

**2.** Cut out carousel top and fold as shown

**3.** Stack plastic or paper cups – put roll of card inside each to build height.

**4.** Circle of card for floor, with surrounding base.

**5.** Fix plastic drinking straws from top to floor.

Make cars, trains or animals to stick on straws – or copy this horse.

# Booth

**1.** Use any size of card tube for base.

**2.** Straws for support.

**3.** Cut section from circle of card as shown. Pull edges together (and stick) to make cone-shaped roof.

**4.** Stick straws to inside of roof and base – and hang up a flag.

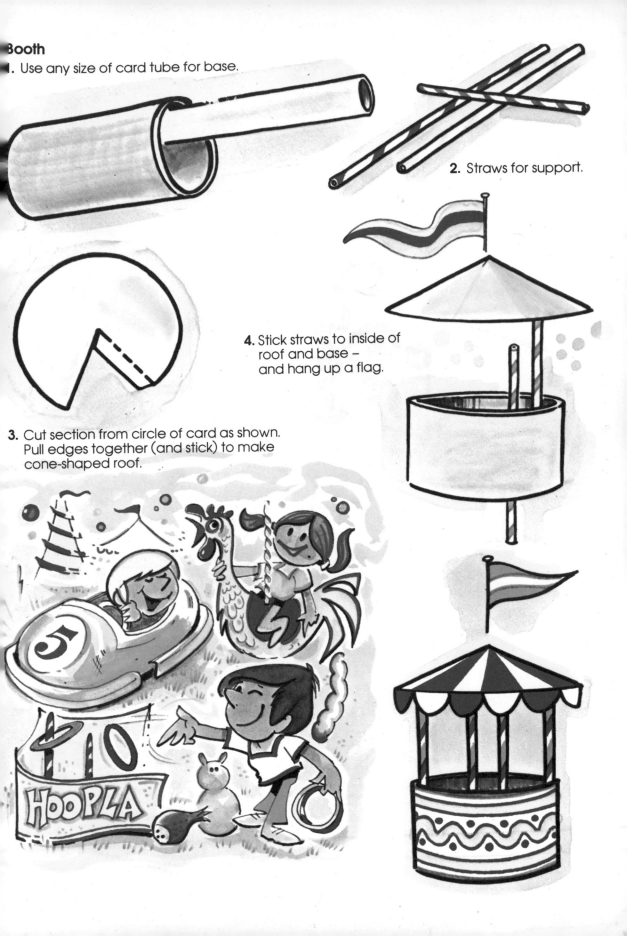

# Doll's House Furniture

You can make all kinds of furniture from things like shoe boxes, matchboxes, polystyrene packaging, cardboard tubes, conkers and acorns. Plus a few pins or nails, some paint, and a little glue.

1. Cut up pieces of a shoe box to make these simple chairs and tables. Paint them bright colours.

2. Use matchbox base as drawer, with paper fastener for handle. Six together with cardboard surround makes chest of drawers.

**3.** Cut cardboard tube as shown. Make seat from flat piece of board. And stick the two together with glue.

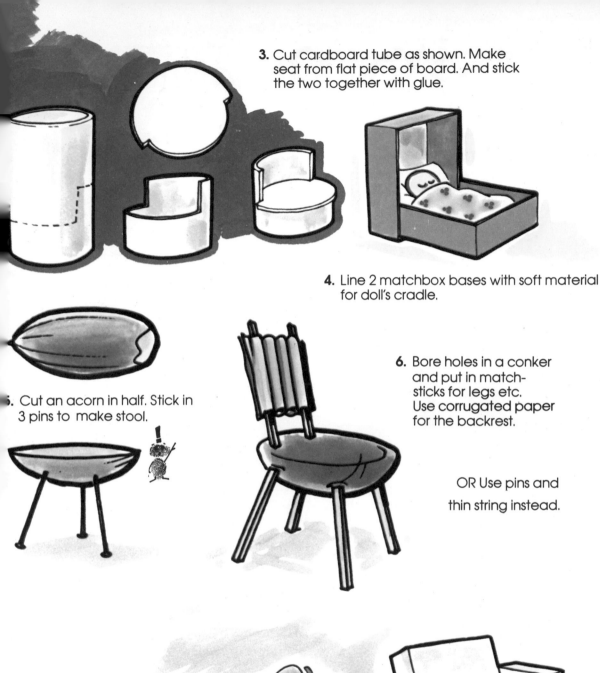

**4.** Line 2 matchbox bases with soft material for doll's cradle.

**6.** Bore holes in a conker and put in matchsticks for legs etc. Use corrugated paper for the backrest.

OR Use pins and thin string instead.

**5.** Cut an acorn in half. Stick in 3 pins to make stool.

**7.** Cut out shapes from polystyrene packaging. If sticking pieces together, use multibond adhesive – other glues could melt it!

# Egging You On

Things to do with eggs and egg boxes.

1. To blow an egg, prick hole with needle at each end. Make sure needle goes in far enough to break yolk. Blow in one hole gently, so that yolk and white are forced out of other end. Don't waste them – use for omelette or scrambled eggs.

2. Cardboard tube makes novel base for egg character. Use paper and wool to decorate.

3. Drip a little oil paint into tray of clean, cold water. Swirl water around until a marble-like pattern appears. Dip egg gently and remove – the pattern will then be on the egg.

4. Decorate egg with latex adhesive, using brush. When absolutely dry, paint egg with dye – or boil in vegetable dye. When dry, peel off latex adhesive (rubber), leaving white pattern on coloured egg.

All these methods are safe.
So you can boil the egg
and eat it afterwards, if you want.

astic egg boxes are made up of interesting shapes.
ut them up with scissors or craft knife and you can make
ll sorts of things – like this bird. Stick the pieces together with
tex adhesive.

Stick top and bottom of egg
compartment together for head.

Button piece for eyes.

2 corners together make body.

**4.** Cut out shapes for beak, tail and legs.

**5.** Make perch from outer edge of box <u>or</u>
from one of the middle sections inside.

**Paint in bright colours.**

# Scrap Art

You can make marvellous pictures and patterns out of almost anything – egg boxes, eggshells, bones (cleaned and dried), rope, cardboard, wood . . . If you use anything metal you must paint it first with rustproof paint – otherwise it will stain.

1. Lay out design on background of chipboard or plywood. Then stick it all down with multibond adhesive.

2. Mix equal amounts of plaster of paris and white powder paint. Add water to make thick, creamy paste. Paint it all over design.

3. You have twenty minutes before paste gets too hard to work. While it's still soft, dab and scratch extra lines and patterns on picture to make it more interesting.

4. Sometimes you can make very attractive pictures from scrap pieces of wood and cardboard without having to cover them with plaster. Like this ship at sea.

# Tree House

If you have a large tree in the garden, or one nearby you can use, try building a tree house – and get a bird's eye-view of life.

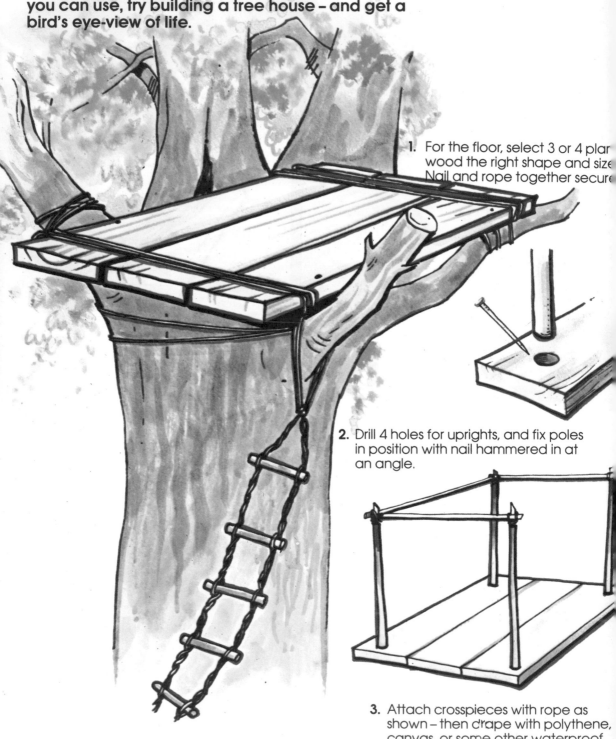

1. For the floor, select 3 or 4 plan wood the right shape and size Nail and rope together secure

2. Drill 4 holes for uprights, and fix poles in position with nail hammered in at an angle.

3. Attach crosspieces with rope as shown – then drape with polythene, canvas, or some other waterproof material for walls and roof.

4. You can make a rope ladder with plaited rope and wooden rungs.

It is easier to make the tree house on the ground, then lift it into the tree.

The most important thing is to make sure it is strong and safe. Get your father or someone to test it before you go up in the world.

# Action Painting

You can make some very interesting patterns with dry sand or paint on the move. But wear your oldest clothes. Ready... Steady... Action!

**1.** Make cone from card, with hole at sharp end. Fix wire handle. Then fill with sand.

**2.** If painting, use a washing-up liquid container – filling it from the bottom.

**3.** String up cone or container as shown.

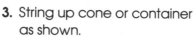

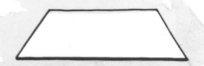

**4.** To change pattern, alter the Y-shape by moving slip knot.

See what patterns you can make with paint when you spill it . . . trickle it . . . or throw it! Then fill in some of the gaps with different colours. But be careful where you do it – and get permission first.

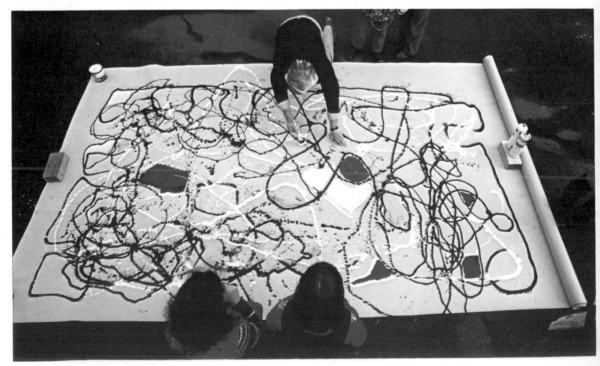

# Chess Men

Make from rolled paper tubes – cartridge paper or thin card
is best. Cut shapes carefully with scissors or craft knife. Stick
with all-purpose glue. Paint them an overall colour – white
and red looks good.

**3.** Castle (2 of each)

**1.** King (1 of each colour)

**2.** Pawn (8 of each)

**4.** Knight (2 of each)

**5.** Bishop (2 of each)

**6.** Queen (1 of each)

**7.** Make chessboard with card, and paint.

# Puppet Shows

Here are three different puppets. Choose one to make, practise hard at working it – then put on a show for the family.

### Glove Puppet

1. Cut hole in ping-pong ball for head (forefinger). Paint face. Add hair or hat.

2. Cardboard gloves for thumb and middle finger – fold and stick.

3. Cover hand with handkerchief.

### Shadow Puppet

1. Make head, arm and body from separate pieces of cardboard. Join with paper fasteners. Wire thin wooden rods to head and arm for movement.

2. Make screen with paper or sheet. Shine light from behind. Audience watch shadows from other side.

# tring Puppet (Marionette)

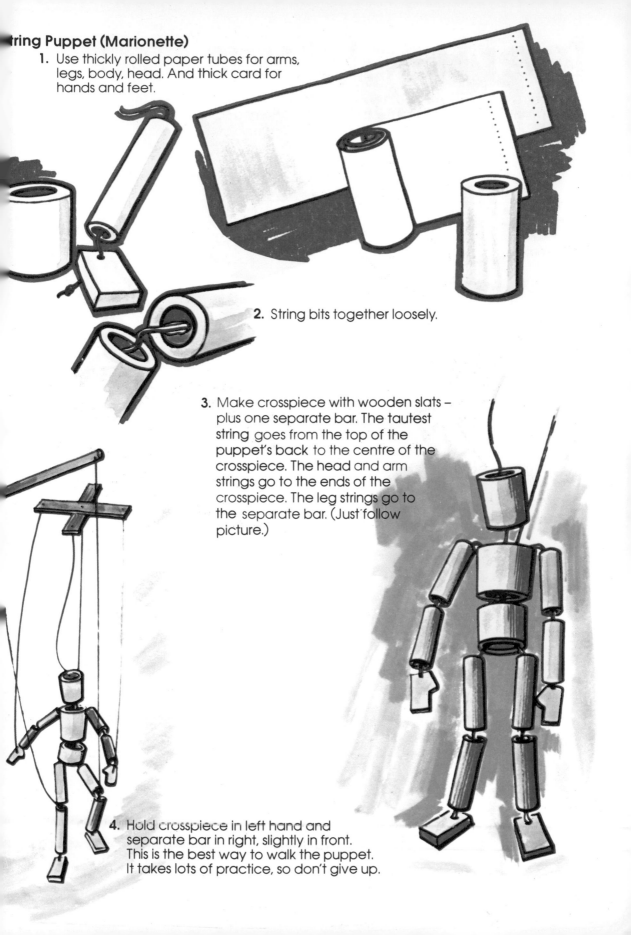

1. Use thickly rolled paper tubes for arms, legs, body, head. And thick card for hands and feet.

2. String bits together loosely.

3. Make crosspiece with wooden slats – plus one separate bar. The tautest string goes from the top of the puppet's back to the centre of the crosspiece. The head and arm strings go to the ends of the crosspiece. The leg strings go to the separate bar. (Just follow picture.)

4. Hold crosspiece in left hand and separate bar in right, slightly in front. This is the best way to walk the puppet. It takes lots of practice, so don't give up.

# Tee! Hee! Shirts

Print your own T-shirt. All you need is a plastic floor tile, some fabric paint, cardboard, something to press with, and . . . a T-shirt.

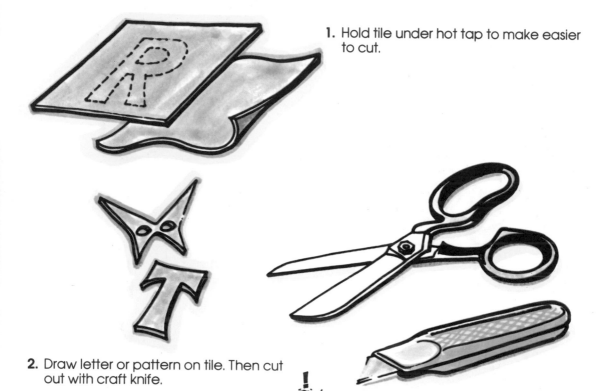

**1.** Hold tile under hot tap to make easier to cut.

**2.** Draw letter or pattern on tile. Then cut out with craft knife.

**3.** Paint reverse side of letter with fabric paint.

**4.** Put piece of cardboard inside T-shirt to keep material stretched – and to stop paint leaking through to the back.

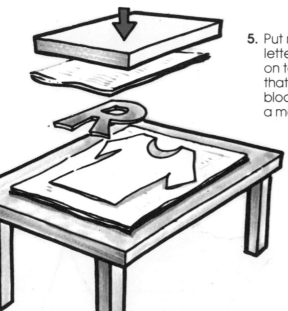

**5.** Put newspaper under T-shirt. Then the letter in position – paint side down – on top. Then more newspaper on top of that. Press very hard – either with heavy block of wood or by putting it through a mangle.

**6.** Take block etc. off very carefully – and hang T-shirt up to dry.

# Wire Sculptures

You make a skeleton of a person or animal – or anything else you like – out of plastic-coated wire. Then build the model on top with clay.

Try getting clay with a nylon fibre in it – it keeps its shape better and is less likely to crack.

When the model is finished you can brush on a coat of hardener, which will make it look and feel as if fired in a kiln – like pottery.

**1.** Twist the wire into shape. Use wire cutters to trim.

**2.** Wrap the clay firmly around the wire.

**3.** Leave one piece of wire uncovered so that you can mount the model on a wooden block. Just make a small hole in the top of the block and stick the wire into it. Make certain it's deep enough, so it doesn't fall over.

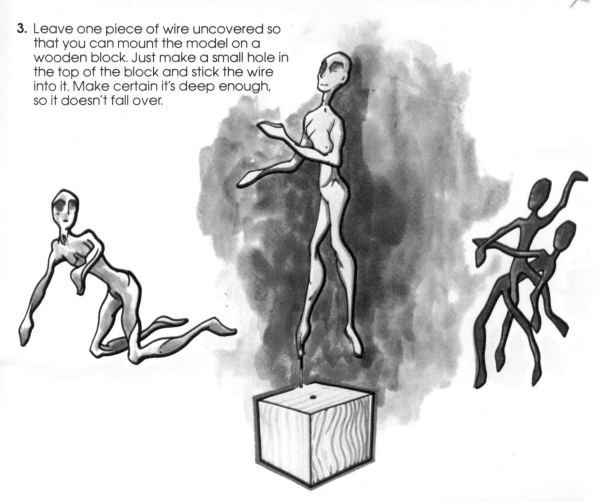

**4.** If you want you can cover the model with metallic paint – to make it look really good.

# Beach Art

Buckets and spades are not the only things for building in the sand. Use boxes or pieces of card and wood to make different shapes and patterns. Decorate with seaweed, driftwood, pebbles and sea-shells.

Make a picture in the sand – draw the lines with a stick and fill in the pattern with shells etc.

*Having a lovely time*

It took these ten children – and me – just one sunny afternoon to make this marvellous picture  All the materials were found on the beach itself. You don't, of course, have to make anything as large as this – small pictures and sculptures can look very good as well. You can have your own beach art gallery. Just use your imagination – and have fun!

# Polystyrenia

Get hold of some polystyrene packaging material. There's lots of it about – ask your local electrical shop for some.

Build a modern city with it. Some of the shapes already look like buildings or towers, others you will want to cut up.

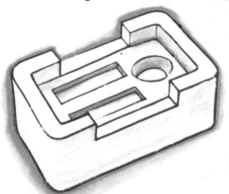

1. Use a craft knife or a proper bread knife. Or, better still, buy a **hot wire**. They come with a small battery and are easy and safe to use. From any tool shop.

2. Stick together with multibond adhesive. Other glues will melt the plastic.

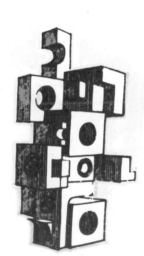

# Treasure Chest

You can make some very unusual jewellery with things like dried peas, peppercorns, holly berries, lentils and macaroni. Great for presents.

1. **Bracelet:** Glue strip of plastic into circlet. Stick on tin foil shapes and dried peas to make pattern. Paint with high gloss modelling paint. If poster paint is used, varnish when dry.

2. **Pendant:** 'Pipe' modelling cement straight from tube onto cardboard. Fix ring fastener, thread with ribbon. Decorate with gold, silver or copper metallic paint.

3. **Brooch:** Glue patterns of seeds, berries etc. onto cardboard. Fix safety pin behind.

**Necklace:** Plait string or plastic-coated wire. Join at ends. Shorter length for matching bracelet.

Paint macaroni, then thread with string.

# Ring Pull Curtains...

Collect lots of ring pulls off drink cans. Link them together by hooking ring of one over tongue of the other. They make interesting curtains – with a nice tinkling sound when the wind blows. But watch out for your fingers, the edges are sharp.

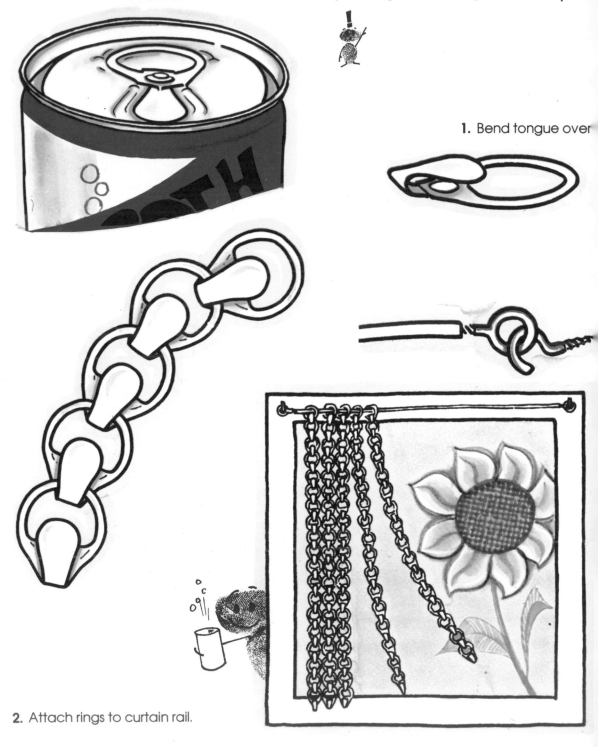

**1.** Bend tongue over

**2.** Attach rings to curtain rail.

# and Thong Things

Get hold of some scrap pieces of leather – ask at your shoe repair shop. You don't need much to make a belt, bracelet, dog lead – or anything else.

**1.** Shape and cut holes in leather with craft knife.

**2.** Fold over and link.

**3.** You can use PVC or other plastic material, as long as it's soft enough to cut and bend.

# Coalminer Doll

When you've made this one think of some other unusual dolls to make. All you need is some felt, a needle and thread, kapok (or some other stuffing), a rubber ball, and some bits and pieces for the trimmings.

Make the doll twice this size – or larger.

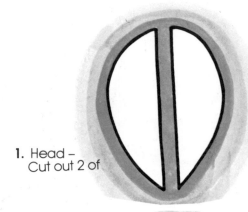

**1.** Head –
Cut out 2 of

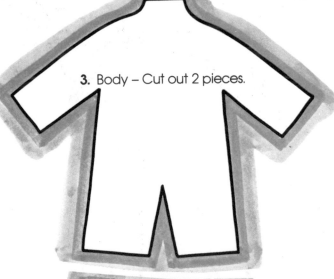

**3.** Body – Cut out 2 pieces.

**2.** Hands – Cut out 2 of each.

**4.** Legs – Cut out 2 of each.

**5.** Foot – Cut out 1 of each.

**6.** Use section of hollow rubber ball for helmet – must be right size to fit head.

**7.** Circle of foil for lamp.
Slice of plastic tubing to stick over foil.
Strip of plastic for belt.
2 pieces of felt for each eye.

**8.** Sew doll together – except head – then turn inside out and stuff with kapok (or bits of old stocking or foam rubber).

**9.** Sew up head, stitch on eyes, and stuff – then sew onto body. Fix helmet, belt and scarf.

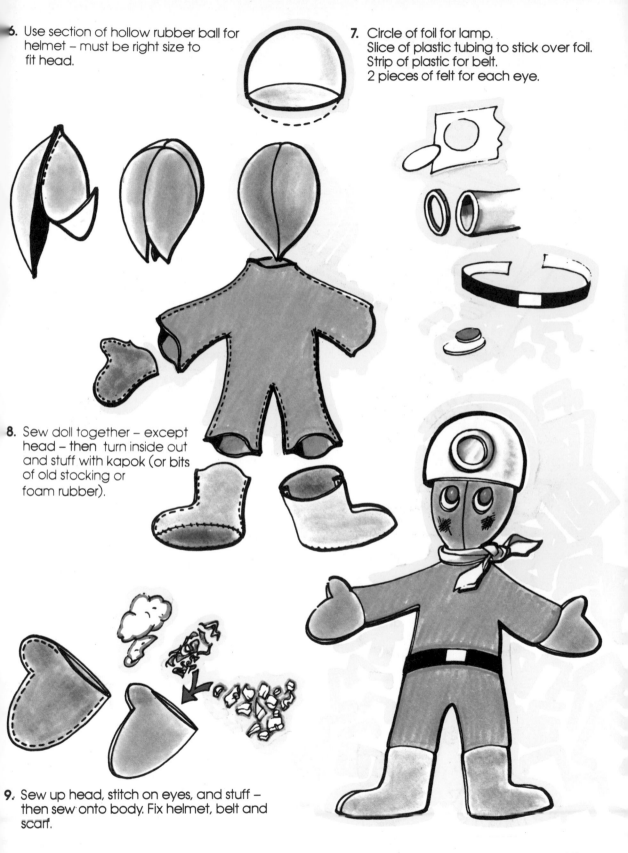

# Pulp Art

You can use papier mâché (pulped paper) for modelling in the same way that you use clay or plasticine. You make it with newspaper – but make sure that Dad's read it first!

1. Tear lots of newspapers into small pieces and put into old saucepan of water – just enough to cover paper.
Bring gently to boil, and stir. Then let mush soak for a while.

2. When lukewarm put in bucket and stir in one tablespoon of cellulose wallpaper adhesive – leave for 15 minutes.

3. The papier mâché is now ready to use. You can make anything you like. If it feels too mushy, squeeze out some liquid.

4. Put your model in warm place, like airing cupboard, to dry.

## Moulds
You can put papier mâché into moulds made of clay, plasticine or plaster to make a model. Faces are always good fun.

1. Make the mould to whatever shape you want, with lots of nice hollows – use these bits and pieces to do it.

2. Then brush it with soapy water – it makes it easier to get the model out afterwards.

3. Fill mould with papier mâché – but don't press too hard if it's plasticine!

4. Test after 6 hours. It shouldn't be completely hard, so you can make last minute adjustments to the shape.

5. When really dry the model can be painted with any sort of paint.

47

# Merry Christmas Decorations

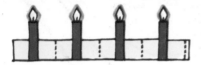

**Cheaper than buying them – and much more fun.**

### 1. Candle Fence:

Cut out shape from cardboard. Fold and stick with all-purpose modelling glue. Use transparent sweet wrappings for 'flames'. Position round candle – but not too close.

### 2. Cards:

Cut out 'windows' on front of card or calendar to reveal your surprise pictures inside.

### 3. Paper Chains:

Draw flat spiral pattern, then cut round carefully. Pull out from centre to make cone – and join a few together.

### 4. Tree:

Bend and join coat-hanger wire – use epoxy resin adhesive. 'Plant' tree in sand or plaster to keep upright.